Table of Contents

Rourke Educational Media
rourkeeducationalmedia.com

Can you find these words?

bones

grass

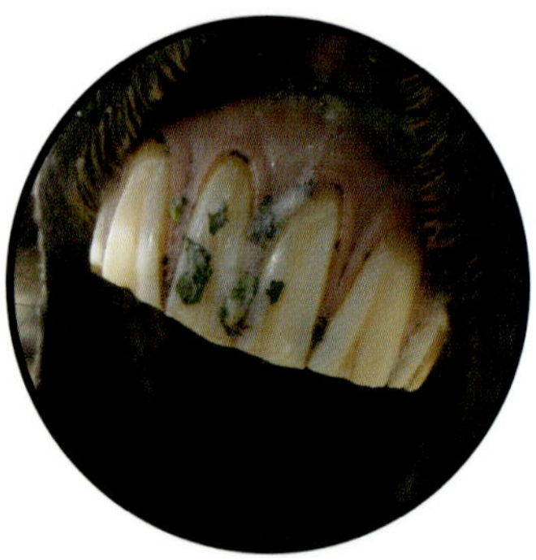

teeth

tusks

Animal Teeth

Animals do not brush their **teeth.**

Elephants dig holes with their **tusks.**

Digging keeps their tusks clean.

Dogs chew **bones**.
Bones clean dogs' teeth.

bone

Cows chew **grass**.

Grass cleans cows' teeth.

Animals drink water.

Water is good for their teeth.

Crocodile teeth fall out.

New, clean teeth grow in!

Did you find these words?

Dogs chew **bones.**

Cows chew **grass.**

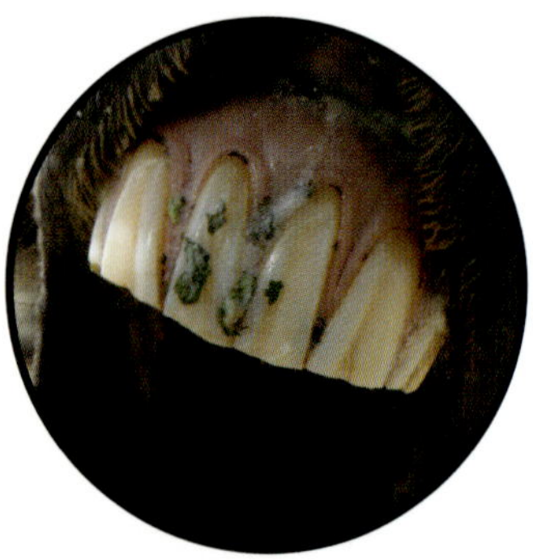

Animals do not brush their **teeth.**

Elephants dig holes with their **tusks.**

Photo Glossary

bones (bohns): The parts of an animal's skeleton.

grass (gras): Plants with leaves that are long, thin blades.

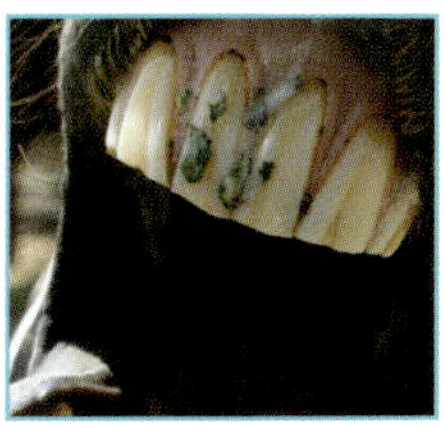

teeth (teeth): The bony parts of the mouth that are used to chew food.

tusks (tuhsks): Long, curved, pointed teeth that stick out of an animal's mouth.

Index

About the Author

Michelle Garcia Andersen lives with her husband, three kids, and lots of pets. She doesn't clean her pets' teeth but she does clean her teeth regularly by brushing and flossing. Michelle has a bit of a sweet tooth so it's really important she takes good care of her teeth.

www.rourkeeducationalmedia.com

PHOTO CREDITS: Cover: ©Top Photo Engineer; p.2,6-7,14,15: ©Mateusz Zagorski; p.2,8-9,14,15: ©Vibrant Image Studio; p.2,3,14,15: ©Heather Pennington; p.2,4-5,14,15: ©Karel Bartik; p.10-11: ©T. Wilbertz; p.12-13: ©Audrey Snider-Bell

Edited by: Keli Sipperley
Cover and interior design by: Rhea Magaro-Wallace

Library of Congress PCN Data
Animal Teeth / Michelle Garcia Andersen
(Let's Find Out)
ISBN (hard cover)(alk. paper) 978-1-64156-190-7
ISBN (soft cover) 978-1-64156-246-1
ISBN (e-Book) 978-1-64156-296-6
Library of Congress Control Number: 2017957800

Printed in the United States of America, North Mankato, Minnesota